Stress-Free Success

Stress-Free Success

Matthew Petchinsky

Stress-Free Success: Achieving Goals Without Anxiety
By: Matthew Petchinsky

Introduction

Stress: the silent killer of success. It creeps into our lives, often unnoticed, until its effects manifest in ways we can no longer ignore. Whether it's the sleepless nights, the unrelenting pressure to perform, or the overwhelming sense of never having enough time, stress infiltrates every corner of our existence. It gnaws away at our ability to think clearly, drains our motivation, and, most devastatingly, prevents us from achieving our full potential.

But why is stress so detrimental to success? At its core, stress creates a mental fog that clouds decision-making, inhibits creativity, and stifles productivity. When your mind is preoccupied with worry or stretched thin by constant demands, it's nearly impossible to focus on what truly matters. You might feel as though you're running a race with no finish line, expending energy but making little meaningful progress. Chronic stress doesn't just slow you down—it erodes your confidence, sabotages your health, and undermines your long-term goals.

The paradox of stress is that it often comes from the very pursuit of success. The drive to achieve more, earn more, or be more can lead to self-imposed expectations that are both unrealistic and unsustainable. Over time, this relentless cycle can leave you feeling stuck, burned out, or even questioning whether the path you're on is worth the toll it's taking.

That's where this guide comes in.

How This Guide Helps You Achieve Without Overwhelm

This guide is not just another productivity manual or self-help book filled with platitudes. It's a carefully curated roadmap designed to help you navigate the challenges of modern life while maintaining your mental and emotional well-being. At its heart, this guide aims to show you that success does not have to come at the expense of your peace of mind.

You'll learn how to identify and combat the hidden stressors that quietly derail your progress. Through actionable strategies, real-world examples, and powerful insights, this guide equips you with tools to create balance, build resilience, and stay focused on what matters most. It's about working smarter, not harder; about aligning your actions with your goals in a way that feels empowering rather than draining.

We'll explore techniques to help you prioritize effectively, set boundaries, and maintain your energy levels. You'll discover how to cultivate a mindset that embraces challenges without succumbing to pressure. Most importantly, you'll gain a clear understanding of how to achieve sustainable success—one that allows you to thrive both personally and professionally.

This guide is a sanctuary in a world that glorifies hustle but overlooks the value of rest and reflection. It's your companion in creating a life where you can achieve your dreams without losing yourself in the process.

The path to success is not a straight line, and it's certainly not without its hurdles. However, with the right tools, mindset, and strategies, you can navigate this journey with clarity and confidence. Let's embark on this transformative journey together, unlocking a future where you achieve greatness not despite the odds, but because you've mastered them—without the weight of stress holding you back.

Welcome to a new way of living, working, and thriving. Let's get started.

Chapter 1: Rethinking Success

Success is one of the most sought-after yet misunderstood concepts in modern life. From an early age, we are conditioned to equate success with external achievements—earning a high income, acquiring material possessions, or gaining recognition in our careers or communities. While these traditional markers of success may bring temporary satisfaction, they often leave us feeling empty, unfulfilled, or even trapped in the relentless pursuit of "more." This chapter is about breaking free from that cycle by rethinking success and redefining it on your own terms.

Defining Success on Your Own Terms

True success is deeply personal. It cannot be dictated by societal norms, family expectations, or cultural pressures. To truly thrive, you must step back and ask yourself, *What does success mean to me?* This question is deceptively simple yet profoundly transformative.

Start by challenging the assumptions you've held about success. Is it tied to a specific job title, a dollar amount in your bank account, or the approval of others? Or is it something more intangible—like the freedom to pursue your passions, the ability to spend quality time with loved ones, or the joy of making a meaningful impact in your community?

Defining success on your own terms involves peeling back layers of external influence to uncover your authentic desires and aspirations. Here are some key steps to guide you:

1. **Reflect on Your Life So Far:**
   Think about moments when you felt truly fulfilled or proud. What were you doing? Who were you with? What values were being honored? These moments often provide clues to your personal definition of success.

2. **Separate Wants from Shoulds:**
   Distinguish between goals that genuinely excite you and those that feel like obligations. For example, you might feel pressure to pursue a high-paying career because it's what society deems successful, but deep down, you might crave a creative or entrepreneurial path.

3. **Visualize Your Ideal Life:**
   Close your eyes and imagine a day in your ideal life. What does it look like? How do you feel? Who are you spending time with? This exercise can help clarify what success looks like for you, free from outside expectations.

4. **Embrace Flexibility:**
   Success is not a static destination; it evolves as you grow and change. Be open to redefining success as your priorities and circumstances shift over time.

By taking ownership of your definition of success, you empower yourself to create a life that feels meaningful and authentic, rather than chasing someone else's version of achievement.

Aligning Goals with Personal Values

Once you've defined what success means to you, the next step is aligning your goals with your personal values. Values are the guiding principles that shape your decisions and give your life purpose. When your goals are in harmony with your values, you experience a sense of fulfillment and alignment. Conversely, when there's a disconnect, you're more likely to feel stressed, unmotivated, or dissatisfied.

Identifying Your Core Values

Your values are deeply rooted in your beliefs and experiences. To identify them, consider the following prompts:

- What qualities do you admire in others?
- What principles do you hold most dear?
- What makes you feel angry or upset when violated?
- What activities or achievements give you a sense of pride or joy?

Common values include integrity, creativity, freedom, family, health, growth, contribution, and adventure. While the list is extensive, narrowing it down to your top five core values will provide clarity and focus.

Aligning Goals with Values

Once you've identified your core values, evaluate your current goals and ask yourself:

- Do these goals reflect what truly matters to me?
- Are my goals driven by external validation, or are they aligned with my internal compass?
- What adjustments can I make to ensure my goals honor my values?

For example, if one of your core values is *freedom*, but your current career path leaves you feeling restricted, you might consider setting a goal to transition to a more flexible role or start your own business. Similarly, if *family* is a top value, you might prioritize spending more quality time with loved ones over taking on extra work commitments.

Creating a Value-Based Goal Framework

To ensure your goals stay aligned with your values, use the following framework:

1. **Clarify Your Why:** For every goal, ask yourself why it matters. This ensures your motivations are rooted in your values rather than external pressures.
2. **Break Goals into Actionable Steps:** Aligning with your values doesn't mean sacrificing ambition—it means pursuing it in a way that feels authentic. Break down your goals into manageable steps that honor your principles.
3. **Evaluate Regularly:** Life is dynamic, and so are your values. Periodically review your goals to ensure they remain aligned with your evolving priorities.

The Benefits of Redefining Success and Aligning Goals

When you redefine success and align your goals with your personal values, several transformative shifts occur:

- **Increased Fulfillment:** You derive deeper satisfaction from your accomplishments because they reflect who you truly are.
- **Reduced Stress:** When your actions are guided by your values, you feel more at peace and less pressured by external expectations.
- **Sustainable Motivation:** Goals that align with your values are inherently motivating, making it easier to stay committed.
- **Greater Resilience:** When challenges arise, your sense of purpose helps you navigate them with clarity and confidence.

A New Perspective on Success

Rethinking success is not about lowering your standards or settling for less. It's about achieving more of what genuinely matters to you. By defining success on your own terms and aligning your goals with your personal values, you unlock a path to success that feels both empowering and sustainable.

As you move forward in this guide, remember that your version of success is valid and worthy, no matter how different it may look from others. Embrace this new perspective and step boldly into a life where your ambitions are fueled by authenticity, not by the silent killer of stress.

Chapter 2: The Calm Planning Framework

Success doesn't happen by accident—it's the result of intentional planning and consistent action. However, the way we approach planning often creates more stress than it alleviates. Rigid schedules, unrealistic timelines, and overpacked to-do lists can leave us feeling overwhelmed and defeated before we've even started. The *Calm Planning Framework* offers a stress-free approach to goal-setting that prioritizes clarity, flexibility, and adaptability, ensuring you achieve your ambitions without sacrificing your peace of mind.

Designing Stress-Free Strategies for Goal-Setting

The foundation of the Calm Planning Framework is its focus on simplicity and sustainability. It's not about doing more; it's about doing what matters most in a way that feels manageable and rewarding. Here's how to design stress-free strategies for your goals:

1. Start with a Vision, Not a To-Do List

Many planning systems begin with a list of tasks, but this approach can quickly become overwhelming. Instead, start by envisioning your desired outcome. Ask yourself:

- What do I want to accomplish?
- Why does this goal matter to me?
- How will achieving this goal improve my life?

By clarifying your vision, you create a compelling "why" that will guide your efforts and keep you motivated.

2. Break Goals into Manageable Milestones

Big goals can feel daunting, which often leads to procrastination or burnout. To avoid this, break your goals into smaller, actionable milestones. For example, if your goal is to write a book, milestones might include:

- Brainstorming and outlining ideas
- Writing one chapter per week
- Editing and revising
- Submitting the manuscript or self-publishing

Each milestone serves as a stepping stone, making your goal feel more achievable and less overwhelming.

3. Prioritize with the 80/20 Rule

The 80/20 rule, also known as the Pareto Principle, states that 80% of your results come from 20% of your efforts. Focus on identifying and prioritizing the tasks that have the greatest impact. Ask yourself:

- Which actions will move me closest to my goal?
- What tasks can I delegate, delay, or eliminate?

By concentrating on high-impact activities, you can achieve more in less time, reducing stress and increasing efficiency.

4. Use Time Blocking for Focus and Balance

Time blocking is a powerful technique that involves scheduling dedicated blocks of time for specific tasks or activities. This method helps you stay focused, avoid multitasking, and create balance in your day. When using time blocking:

- Reserve time for high-priority tasks during your peak energy hours.
- Schedule breaks to recharge and prevent burnout.
- Include time for self-care, hobbies, and relationships to maintain overall well-being.

5. Plan for Energy, Not Just Time

Traditional planning focuses on managing your time, but managing your energy is equally important. Pay attention to when you feel most alert and productive, and plan demanding tasks during these periods. Similarly, schedule lighter tasks or breaks during low-energy times to maintain a sustainable pace.

The Importance of Flexibility and Adaptability

No matter how well you plan, life is unpredictable. Unexpected challenges, opportunities, or changes in circumstances can derail even the most meticulously crafted plans. That's why flexibility and adaptability are essential components of the Calm Planning Framework.

1. Embrace the Concept of Fluid Goals

Rigid goals can become a source of frustration when circumstances change. Instead, think of your goals as fluid—capable of evolving as you gain new insights or face unforeseen obstacles. This doesn't mean abandoning your goals; it means being open to adjusting your approach while staying true to your vision.

2. Build Buffers into Your Plans

One of the most common sources of stress is overestimating what you can accomplish in a given timeframe. To avoid this, build buffers into your plans. For example:

- Schedule extra time for tasks to account for delays or interruptions.
- Include "catch-up" days in your calendar to address unfinished work.
- Avoid overcommitting by saying "no" to activities that don't align with your priorities.

Buffers create breathing room, giving you the flexibility to adapt without feeling overwhelmed.

3. Develop a Resilience Mindset

Adaptability begins with mindset. Instead of seeing setbacks as failures, view them as opportunities to learn and grow. When things don't go as planned, ask yourself:

- What can I learn from this experience?
- How can I adjust my plan to move forward?

- What resources or support do I need to overcome this challenge?

By cultivating resilience, you can navigate change with confidence and grace.

4. Regularly Review and Adjust Your Plans

Effective planning is an ongoing process, not a one-time event. Set aside time to regularly review your goals and progress. During these check-ins:

- Celebrate your accomplishments to stay motivated.
- Reassess your priorities to ensure they align with your values and vision.
- Make adjustments to your plans as needed, based on new information or circumstances.

These reviews keep your plans dynamic and relevant, allowing you to stay on track without unnecessary stress.

The Benefits of the Calm Planning Framework

The Calm Planning Framework is designed to help you achieve your goals in a way that feels sustainable and empowering. Here are some key benefits:

1. **Reduced Overwhelm:** By focusing on manageable milestones and high-impact tasks, you avoid the pressure of tackling everything at once.
2. **Improved Focus:** Time blocking and energy management help you work smarter, not harder, so you can make meaningful progress without distractions.
3. **Greater Flexibility:** The emphasis on adaptability ensures you can handle unexpected changes without losing momentum.
4. **Enhanced Well-Being:** Incorporating self-care and balance into your plans prevents burnout and supports your overall mental and emotional health.

Planning for Success Without the Stress

The Calm Planning Framework is not about achieving perfection; it's about creating a sustainable path to success that honors your values, priorities, and well-being. By designing stress-free strategies and embracing flexibility, you can approach your goals with confidence and ease, knowing that you're prepared for whatever challenges or opportunities come your way.

As you move forward in this guide, remember that planning is a tool to support your journey, not a rigid script you must follow. Use the Calm Planning Framework as a foundation to build a life of purpose, progress, and peace.

Chapter 3: Handling High-Stress Moments

No matter how well you plan or how aligned your goals are with your values, high-stress moments are inevitable. Life's unpredictability can bring challenges that feel overwhelming, whether it's an unexpected deadline, a conflict with a loved one, or a major life decision. What matters most is how you respond in these moments. This chapter equips you with tools and techniques to stay calm under pressure and regain control, allowing you to navigate even the most intense situations with grace and clarity.

Tools for Staying Calm Under Pressure

High-stress moments often trigger a fight-or-flight response, making it difficult to think clearly or make rational decisions. To handle these moments effectively, it's essential to have tools that help you stay grounded, focused, and composed.

1. Pause and Assess the Situation

When stress hits, your first instinct might be to react immediately. However, taking a moment to pause and assess the situation can prevent impulsive decisions. Ask yourself:

- What is happening right now?
- What is within my control?
- What is the most urgent priority?

This quick assessment helps you shift from a reactive state to a proactive mindset, allowing you to respond thoughtfully instead of letting stress dictate your actions.

2. Focus on What You Can Control

Stress often arises from situations that feel beyond your control. By identifying the aspects you can influence, you can redirect your energy toward productive actions. For example:

- If you're overwhelmed by a tight deadline, focus on completing one task at a time rather than worrying about the entire project.
- If you're facing a conflict, concentrate on how you communicate and respond rather than trying to control the other person's behavior.

Recognizing your sphere of control helps you regain a sense of agency, reducing feelings of helplessness.

3. Break the Situation into Manageable Steps

High-stress moments can make problems seem insurmountable. Breaking the situation into smaller, manageable steps can make it feel less daunting. Create a quick action plan by asking:

- What is the first thing I can do right now?
- What resources or support do I need?
- What is the next logical step after that?

Progress, even in small increments, helps to alleviate stress and build momentum.

4. Use Visualization to Regain Perspective

Visualization is a powerful tool for staying calm under pressure. Close your eyes and imagine yourself successfully handling the situation. Picture the steps you'll take, the positive outcome you'll achieve, and how you'll feel afterward. This exercise not only reduces anxiety but also boosts your confidence and focus.

5. Leverage Support Systems

You don't have to handle high-stress moments alone. Reach out to trusted friends, family members, or colleagues who can provide perspective, encouragement, or practical assistance. Simply talking through your challenges can help you process your emotions and develop a clearer plan of action.

6. Practice Self-Compassion

In high-stress moments, it's easy to be hard on yourself, but self-criticism only adds to the pressure. Instead, practice self-compassion by acknowledging your feelings and reminding yourself that it's okay to struggle. Replace negative self-talk with affirmations like:

- "I am doing the best I can."
- "This is a tough moment, but I can handle it."
- "I will take this one step at a time."

Breathing and Grounding Techniques

When stress escalates, your body's physiological response can make it difficult to think clearly or remain calm. Breathing and grounding techniques are essential tools for resetting your nervous system and regaining a sense of control.

1. Deep Breathing Exercises

Deep breathing is one of the most effective ways to calm your body and mind. By slowing your breath, you signal to your brain that it's safe to relax. Here are three simple techniques:

- **Box Breathing:**
    1. Inhale for a count of 4.
    2. Hold your breath for a count of 4.
    3. Exhale for a count of 4.
    4. Hold your breath again for a count of 4.
       Repeat this cycle for 2–5 minutes to lower your heart rate and reduce anxiety.
- **4-7-8 Breathing:**
    1. Inhale through your nose for 4 seconds.
    2. Hold your breath for 7 seconds.
    3. Exhale through your mouth for 8 seconds.
       This technique is particularly effective for calming your mind before making important decisions or preparing for sleep.
- **Alternate Nostril Breathing:**
    1. Close your right nostril with your thumb and inhale deeply through your left nostril.
    2. Close your left nostril with your ring finger and exhale through your right nostril.

3. Inhale through your right nostril, then switch and exhale through your left nostril.
   Alternate for 1–3 minutes to promote balance and relaxation.

2. Grounding Techniques for Immediate Relief

Grounding techniques are designed to anchor you in the present moment, helping to alleviate feelings of overwhelm or panic.

- **The 5-4-3-2-1 Method:**
    1. Name 5 things you can see.
    2. Name 4 things you can touch.
    3. Name 3 things you can hear.
    4. Name 2 things you can smell.
    5. Name 1 thing you can taste.
       This sensory exercise shifts your focus from stress to your immediate environment, grounding you in the present.
- **Progressive Muscle Relaxation:**
    1. Start at your feet and slowly tense each muscle group for 5 seconds, then release.
    2. Work your way up through your legs, torso, arms, and face. This technique relieves physical tension and promotes a sense of calm.
- **Holding a Comfort Object:**
  Keep a small, meaningful item like a smooth stone, piece of jewelry, or fabric with you. When stress strikes, hold the object and focus on its texture, weight, and significance. This simple action can provide a sense of stability.

3. Nature-Based Grounding

Spending time in nature or visualizing natural settings can have a calming effect. If possible, step outside and focus on the feeling of the ground beneath your feet, the sound of birds, or the rustling of leaves. If you can't go outside, close your eyes and imagine a peaceful natural setting, such as a forest, beach, or meadow.

Putting It All Together

Handling high-stress moments is about having the right tools and mindset to manage pressure effectively. By pausing, focusing on what you can control, and using techniques like deep breathing and grounding, you can regain clarity and composure when it matters most.

Stress doesn't have to derail your progress or dominate your life. With practice, these techniques will become second nature, allowing you to face challenges with confidence and resilience.

Chapter 4: The Balance Blueprint

In the pursuit of success, many of us fall into the trap of overworking ourselves, neglecting rest and personal time in the process. The result? Burnout—a state of physical, emotional, and mental exhaustion that undermines our health, happiness, and productivity. Achieving true success requires balance: the art of harmonizing work, rest, and personal time. This chapter introduces the *Balance Blueprint*, a framework for cultivating a fulfilling and sustainable lifestyle that protects against burnout while enabling you to thrive.

Balancing Work, Rest, and Personal Time

Modern life often demands that we wear multiple hats: employee, entrepreneur, partner, parent, friend, and more. Balancing these roles requires intentionality and discipline, as it's easy to let one area of life overshadow the others. The key to balance lies in prioritizing what matters most and allocating your time and energy accordingly.

1. Understand Your Priorities

Balance begins with clarity about what's truly important to you. Take a moment to reflect on the following questions:

- What are my top priorities in life (e.g., career, family, health, personal growth)?
- How much time and energy am I currently dedicating to each of these areas?
- Are there any areas I'm neglecting that need more attention?

Once you've identified your priorities, you can begin to allocate your time in a way that aligns with your values and goals.

2. Embrace Time Blocking

Time blocking is a powerful technique for creating balance in your daily routine. By scheduling specific blocks of time for work, rest, and personal activities, you ensure that each area of your life gets the attention it deserves. Here's how to implement time blocking effectively:

- **Work:** Dedicate focused blocks of time to your most important tasks. Eliminate distractions during these periods to maximize productivity.
- **Rest:** Schedule regular breaks throughout the day to recharge. These can include short walks, power naps, or moments of mindfulness.
- **Personal Time:** Set aside time for activities that bring you joy and fulfillment, such as hobbies, exercise, or spending time with loved ones.

3. Set Boundaries

Boundaries are essential for maintaining balance. Without them, it's easy for work or other responsibilities to spill over into your personal time, leaving you feeling drained. Here are some practical ways to establish boundaries:

- **Work Boundaries:** Avoid checking emails or taking work calls outside of your designated work hours. Communicate your boundaries clearly to colleagues and clients.
- **Personal Boundaries:** Say "no" to commitments that don't align with your priorities or values. Protect your time and energy for what truly matters.
- **Technology Boundaries:** Limit screen time, especially in the evenings, to create space for relaxation and connection.

4. Balance Over Time, Not Perfection

Balance doesn't mean achieving a perfectly equal distribution of time every day. Some days, work may require more focus; other days, personal or family commitments may take precedence. Strive for balance over the course of a week or month, rather than expecting it to happen daily.

Avoiding Burnout Through Self-Care Practices

Burnout is a significant risk when you consistently push yourself beyond your limits without taking time to recharge. Self-care is not a luxury—it's a necessity for maintaining your physical, emotional, and mental well-being.

1. Prioritize Physical Health

Your body is the foundation of your energy and productivity. Taking care of your physical health helps you stay resilient and focused. Key practices include:

- **Regular Exercise:** Engage in physical activity that you enjoy, whether it's walking, yoga, dancing, or weightlifting. Aim for at least 30 minutes of movement most days.
- **Nutritious Diet:** Fuel your body with whole, nutrient-dense foods that provide sustained energy. Stay hydrated and limit caffeine and sugar.
- **Quality Sleep:** Prioritize 7–9 hours of sleep each night. Establish a consistent bedtime routine and create a sleep-friendly environment by keeping your bedroom cool, dark, and quiet.

2. Foster Emotional Well-Being

Your emotional health plays a critical role in preventing burnout. Practices that support emotional well-being include:

- **Journaling:** Write about your thoughts and feelings to process emotions and gain clarity.
- **Therapy or Counseling:** Seek professional support if you're feeling overwhelmed or struggling with persistent stress.
- **Gratitude Practice:** Take a few minutes each day to reflect on what you're grateful for. Gratitude shifts your focus from stress to positivity.

3. Cultivate Mental Resilience

High-stress moments and challenges are inevitable, but building mental resilience can help you navigate them effectively. Consider these practices:

- **Mindfulness Meditation:** Spend 5–10 minutes each day focusing on your breath or a calming visualization. This practice reduces stress and improves focus.
- **Stress Management Techniques:** Use breathing exercises, grounding techniques, or progressive muscle relaxation to manage acute stress.
- **Continuous Learning:** Engage in activities that stimulate your mind, such as reading, puzzles, or learning a new skill.

4. Nurture Social Connections

Strong relationships provide emotional support and a sense of belonging, both of which are essential for combating burnout. Make time to connect with loved ones, whether it's through a phone call, a shared meal, or a fun activity. Surround yourself with people who uplift and inspire you.

5. Schedule Regular Self-Care Rituals

Incorporate self-care into your routine as a non-negotiable practice. Examples include:

- A weekly spa night or bubble bath.
- A daily walk in nature.
- A monthly "me day" where you indulge in activities you love.

The Benefits of Balance and Self-Care

Implementing the *Balance Blueprint* and prioritizing self-care offers a host of benefits:

1. **Increased Energy:** When you rest and recharge regularly, you have more energy to devote to your goals.
2. **Improved Focus:** A balanced lifestyle enhances your ability to concentrate and think clearly.
3. **Greater Resilience:** Self-care builds the physical and emotional reserves you need to handle stress and challenges.
4. **Enhanced Relationships:** By making time for personal connections, you strengthen your support system and foster deeper bonds.
5. **Sustainable Success:** Balance prevents burnout, allowing you to achieve your ambitions without sacrificing your well-being.

Designing Your Balance Blueprint

Creating balance is an ongoing process that requires self-awareness and adaptability. Use the following steps to design your personalized Balance Blueprint:

1. **Assess Your Current Balance:** Identify areas where you're over-committed or neglecting important aspects of your life.
2. **Set Intentions:** Define what balance looks like for you and set clear intentions for achieving it.
3. **Experiment and Adjust:** Try different strategies to find what works best for you. Be willing to make adjustments as your priorities and circumstances change.

A Life of Harmony and Fulfillment

The *Balance Blueprint* is more than a framework—it's a philosophy for living a life of harmony and fulfillment. By balancing work, rest, and personal time and incorporating self-care into your routine, you can avoid burnout and create a lifestyle that supports both your ambitions and your well-being.

Chapter 5: Sustaining Stress-Free Success

Achieving success is one thing; sustaining it without succumbing to stress is another. Many people work hard to reach their goals, only to burn out once they've arrived. Sustaining stress-free success requires a deliberate approach to managing your mindset, setting up systems of support, and fostering habits that promote resilience and balance. This chapter provides a roadmap for maintaining a low-stress mindset and building a network that empowers you to grow and thrive over the long term.

Maintaining a Low-Stress Mindset for Long-Term Goals

Your mindset is the foundation of how you approach challenges, opportunities, and the journey toward your goals. A low-stress mindset doesn't mean avoiding challenges altogether—it means cultivating the mental tools to handle them effectively.

1. Embrace a Growth Mindset

A growth mindset, as defined by psychologist Carol Dweck, is the belief that your abilities and intelligence can be developed through effort and learning. This mindset fosters resilience, adaptability, and a positive outlook on challenges.

To develop a growth mindset:

- View setbacks as opportunities to learn rather than as failures.
- Focus on effort and progress rather than perfection.
- Celebrate small victories to reinforce your belief in your ability to grow.

2. Practice Mindfulness to Stay Present

Stress often arises from dwelling on past mistakes or worrying about future uncertainties. Mindfulness anchors you in the present, allowing you to focus on what you can control in the moment.

Simple mindfulness practices include:

- Starting your day with a 5-minute meditation.
- Taking a few deep breaths whenever you feel overwhelmed.
- Practicing gratitude by reflecting on three things you're thankful for each day.

3. Reframe Stress as a Challenge, Not a Threat

Stress is often perceived as a negative force, but reframing it as a challenge can make it a motivating factor. Instead of thinking, *"This is too much for me,"* try thinking, *"This is an opportunity to grow and prove my capabilities."*

When faced with a stressful situation:

- Break it down into manageable steps.
- Focus on the aspects you can control.
- Remind yourself of past challenges you've successfully overcome.

4. Set Realistic Expectations

Unrealistic expectations are a breeding ground for stress. Avoid setting yourself up for disappointment by being honest about what you can achieve within a given timeframe.

- **Set SMART Goals:** Goals should be Specific, Measurable, Achievable, Relevant, and Time-bound.
- **Be Kind to Yourself:** Understand that success takes time and that setbacks are part of the process.

5. Schedule Regular Reflection and Adjustment

Long-term success requires regular check-ins to evaluate your progress and adjust your strategies. Take time each week or month to reflect on questions like:

- Are my goals still aligned with my values?
- What's working well, and what needs to change?
- Am I maintaining a balance between work, rest, and personal time?

This habit of reflection keeps you on track while preventing unnecessary stress from building up.

Building a Support Network for Growth

No one achieves lasting success alone. A strong support network provides encouragement, accountability, and resources to help you overcome challenges and seize opportunities. Here's how to build and nurture a network that supports your growth.

1. Identify Key Support Roles

Your support network should include people who fulfill different roles in your journey. These may include:

- **Mentors:** Individuals who have experience in your field and can offer guidance and advice.
- **Peers:** Colleagues or friends who are pursuing similar goals and can share insights and encouragement.
- **Cheerleaders:** Supportive friends or family members who believe in you and celebrate your successes.
- **Accountability Partners:** People who hold you accountable for your commitments and help you stay on track.

2. Foster Meaningful Connections

Building a strong support network requires effort and authenticity. Focus on developing genuine relationships by:

- **Listening Actively:** Show interest in others' goals and challenges.
- **Offering Help:** Be willing to support others in their endeavors.
- **Expressing Gratitude:** Thank those who support you and acknowledge their contributions.

3. Leverage Technology for Connection

In today's digital world, your support network doesn't have to be limited to people you interact with in person. Use technology to:

- Join online communities related to your field or interests.
- Attend virtual networking events or webinars.
- Stay connected with mentors, peers, and friends through video calls, emails, or social media.

4. Seek Professional Support When Needed

Sometimes, the best way to sustain success is by seeking help from professionals. This might include:

- **Coaches or Consultants:** Experts who can help you refine your strategies and overcome obstacles.
- **Therapists or Counselors:** Professionals who can provide emotional support and tools for managing stress.
- **Financial Advisors:** Specialists who can help you make informed decisions about your resources and investments.

5. Create a Culture of Support

Support networks thrive when they are reciprocal. By offering support to others, you create a culture of mutual growth and encouragement. Share your knowledge, celebrate others' achievements, and be a source of positivity in your community.

Sustaining Success Over the Long Term

Sustaining stress-free success is not about avoiding challenges but about building the resilience and support needed to navigate them. By maintaining a low-stress mindset and surrounding yourself with a strong network, you can continue to grow and achieve your goals without sacrificing your well-being.

Key takeaways from this chapter include:

1. Cultivating a growth mindset to approach challenges with confidence and curiosity.
2. Practicing mindfulness and reframing stress to stay present and focused.
3. Building a diverse support network that provides guidance, encouragement, and accountability.
4. Regularly reflecting on your progress and making adjustments to stay aligned with your values and goals.

Success is a journey, not a destination. By adopting these strategies, you can enjoy the process and sustain your achievements for years to come.

Appendix A: Guided Exercises for Calm Goal Achievement

This appendix provides a collection of guided exercises to help you implement the strategies from this guide and achieve your goals without stress. Each exercise is designed to enhance clarity, focus, and resilience while keeping you grounded and balanced. Use these exercises regularly to maintain a calm approach to success.

Exercise 1: The Vision Clarity Exercise

Purpose: To create a clear and motivating vision for your goals.

1. **Find a Quiet Space:** Sit in a comfortable position where you won't be disturbed. Close your eyes and take a few deep breaths to center yourself.

2. **Visualize Your Ideal Outcome:** Picture your goal as if it has already been achieved. Imagine the details:
   - What does success look like?
   - How do you feel?
   - Who is celebrating with you?

3. **Engage All Your Senses:**
   - What do you see, hear, smell, taste, and feel in this moment of success?
   - Make the vision as vivid as possible.

4. **Reflect and Write:** Open your eyes and write down your vision. Include as many details as possible. This will serve as your north star when setting and pursuing goals.

Exercise 2: The SMART Goals Worksheet
Purpose: To break down your goals into actionable, stress-free steps.

1. **Define Your Goal:** Write down the goal you want to achieve.
2. **Make It SMART:** Break it down using the SMART framework:
   - **Specific:** What exactly do you want to achieve?
   - **Measurable:** How will you measure your progress?
   - **Achievable:** Is the goal realistic given your current resources and time?
   - **Relevant:** Does this goal align with your values and long-term vision?
   - **Time-bound:** What is your deadline for achieving this goal?
3. **Outline Steps:** List the major steps needed to accomplish the goal. Break these into smaller tasks where possible.
4. **Review:** Reassess the goal to ensure it feels manageable and aligned with your priorities.

Exercise 3: The Daily Prioritization Practice
Purpose: To focus on high-impact tasks each day.

1. **Start with a Brain Dump:** Spend 5 minutes writing down everything you need or want to do.
2. **Categorize Tasks:** Group your tasks into three categories:
    - **High Priority:** Tasks that directly contribute to your goals.
    - **Medium Priority:** Tasks that are important but not urgent.
    - **Low Priority:** Tasks that can be delegated, delayed, or eliminated.
3. **Choose Your Top 3:** From the high-priority category, select three tasks to focus on today.
4. **Time Block:** Allocate specific times in your day to complete these tasks.
5. **Reflect:** At the end of the day, review your progress and celebrate what you accomplished.

Exercise 4: The Stress Reframing Practice
Purpose: To shift your perspective on stressful situations.

1. **Identify the Stressor:** Write down the situation or challenge causing you stress.
2. **Examine Your Thoughts:** What thoughts or beliefs are contributing to your stress? Write them down.
3. **Reframe the Situation:** Ask yourself:
    - What can I learn from this challenge?
    - How can I grow from this experience?
    - What is within my control right now?
4. **Create an Affirmation:** Turn your reframed perspective into a positive affirmation. For example, "I am capable of handling this challenge with confidence and clarity."

Exercise 5: The Gratitude Reset

Purpose: To cultivate a positive mindset and reduce stress.

1. **Set Aside 5 Minutes:** Find a quiet space and take a few deep breaths to center yourself.
2. **Reflect on Your Day:** Think about three things you're grateful for today. These can be big or small, such as a kind gesture from a friend or completing a task.
3. **Write It Down:** Record your gratitude list in a journal. Include why each item is meaningful to you.
4. **Feel the Gratitude:** Close your eyes and focus on the positive feelings associated with each item on your list. Let these feelings fill you with calm and joy.

Exercise 6: Grounding for Calm Clarity

Purpose: To center yourself during overwhelming moments.

1. **Find a Quiet Spot:** Sit comfortably with your feet flat on the ground.
2. **5-4-3-2-1 Grounding:**
   - Name 5 things you can see around you.
   - Name 4 things you can touch.
   - Name 3 things you can hear.
   - Name 2 things you can smell.
   - Name 1 thing you can taste.
3. **Focus on Your Breath:** Take slow, deep breaths as you complete the exercise.

This technique helps shift your focus away from stress and brings you into the present moment.

Exercise 7: Monthly Goal Reflection and Adjustment
Purpose: To evaluate progress and adjust your strategies.

1. **Review Your Goals:** Look back at the goals you set for the month.
2. **Assess Progress:** Ask yourself:
    ◦ What did I accomplish?
    ◦ What challenges did I face?
    ◦ What worked well, and what didn't?
3. **Refine Your Approach:** Based on your reflections, adjust your goals or strategies for the next month.
4. **Celebrate Wins:** Acknowledge and celebrate your successes, no matter how small.

Exercise 8: Self-Care Scheduling
Purpose: To incorporate self-care into your routine.

1. **List Your Favorite Self-Care Activities:** Examples might include reading, exercise, meditation, or spending time with loved ones.
2. **Schedule It In:** Use a planner or calendar to block time for at least one self-care activity each day.
3. **Honor the Commitment:** Treat self-care as a non-negotiable priority, just like a work meeting or appointment.

Exercise 9: Visualization for Overcoming Challenges
Purpose: To build confidence and reduce anxiety about upcoming challenges.

1. **Choose a Challenge:** Identify a specific challenge you're currently facing.
2. **Visualize Success:** Close your eyes and imagine yourself successfully navigating the challenge. Picture the steps you'll take and the positive outcome you'll achieve.
3. **Focus on Feelings:** Pay attention to how confident and calm you feel in this visualization.
4. **Revisit as Needed:** Use this visualization technique whenever you need a boost of confidence or clarity.

Exercise 10: The Energy Audit
Purpose: To manage your energy and avoid burnout.

1. **Track Your Energy Levels:** For one week, record how your energy fluctuates throughout the day.
2. **Identify Patterns:** Note when you feel most energized and when you feel drained.
3. **Adjust Your Schedule:** Align demanding tasks with high-energy periods and lighter activities with low-energy times.
4. **Incorporate Recharge Breaks:** Schedule breaks to rest and recharge during your low-energy periods.

These exercises form the foundation of a calm and balanced approach to goal achievement. By incorporating them into your routine, you'll build the resilience and focus needed to sustain success without stress. Revisit this appendix whenever you need a practical tool to stay on track and maintain your well-being.

<u>Message from the Author:</u>

I hope you enjoyed this book, I love astrology and knew there was not a book such as this out on the shelf. I love metaphysical items as well. Please check out my other books:

-Life of Government Benefits

-My life of Hell

-My life with Hydrocephalus

-Red Sky

-World Domination:Woman's rule

-World Domination:Woman's Rule 2: The War

-Life and Banishment of Apophis: book 1

-The Kidney Friendly Diet

-The Ultimate Hemp Cookbook

-Creating a Dispensary(legally)

-Cleanliness throughout life: the importance of showering from childhood to adulthood.

-Strong Roots: The Risks of Overcoddling children

-Hemp Horoscopes: Cosmic Insights and Earthly Healing

- Celestial Hemp Navigating the Zodiac: Through the Green Cosmos

-Astrological Hemp: Aligning The Stars with Earth's Ancient Herb

-The Astrological Guide to Hemp: Stars, Signs, and Sacred Leaves

-Green Growth: Innovative Marketing Strategies for your Hemp Products and Dispensary

-Cosmic Cannabis

-Astrological Munchies

-Henry The Hemp

-Zodiacal Roots: The Astrological Soul Of Hemp

- **Green Constellations: Intersection of Hemp and Zodiac**

-Hemp in The Houses: An astrological Adventure Through The Cannabis Galaxy

-Galactic Ganja Guide

Heavenly Hemp

Zodiac Leaves

Doctor Who Astrology

Cannastrology

Stellar Satvias and Cosmic Indicas

Celestial Cannabis: A Zodiac Journey

AstroHerbology: The Sky and The Soil: Volume 1

AstroHerbology:Celestial Cannabis:Volume 2

Cosmic Cannabis Cultivation

The Starry Guide to Herbal Harmony: Volume 1

The Starry Guide to Herbal Harmony: Cannabis Universe: Volume 2

Yugioh Astrology: Astrological Guide to Deck, Duels and more

Nightmare Mansion: Echoes of The Abyss

Nightmare Mansion 2: Legacy of Shadows

Nightmare Mansion 3: Shadows of the Forgotten

Nightmare Mansion 4: Echoes of the Damned

The Life and Banishment of Apophis: Book 2

Nightmare Mansion: Halls of Despair

Healing with Herb: Cannabis and Hydrocephalus

Planetary Pot: Aligning with Astrological Herbs: Volume 1

Fast Track to Freedom: 30 Days to Financial Independence Using AI, Assets, and Agile Hustles

Cosmic Hemp Pathways

How to Become Financially Free in 30 Days: 10,000 Paths to Prosperity

Zodiacal Herbage: Astrological Insights: Volume 1

Nightmare Mansion: Whispers in the Walls

The Daleks Invade Atlantis

Henry the hemp and Hydrocephalus

10X The Kidney Friendly Diet
Cannabis Universe: Adult coloring book
Hemp Astrology: The Healing Power of the Stars
Zodiacal Herbage: Astrological Insights: Cannabis Universe: Volume 2
<u>**Planetary Pot: Aligning with Astrological Herbs: Cannabis Universes: Volume 2**</u>
Doctor Who Meets the Replicators and SG-1: The Ultimate Battle for Survival
Nightmare Mansion: Curse of the Blood Moon
<u>**The Celestial Stoner: A Guide to the Zodiac**</u>
Cosmic Pleasures: Sex Toy Astrology for Every Sign
Hydrocephalus Astrology: Navigating the Stars and Healing Waters
Lapis and the Mischievous Chocolate Bar

Celestial Positions: Sexual Astrology for Every Sign
Apophis's Shadow Work Journal: : A Journey of Self-Discovery and Healing
Kinky Cosmos: Sexual Kink Astrology for Every Sign
Digital Cosmos: The Astrological Digimon Compendium
Stellar Seeds: The Cosmic Guide to Growing with Astrology
Apophis's Daily Gratitude Journal

Cat Astrology: Feline Mysteries of the Cosmos
The Cosmic Kama Sutra: An Astrological Guide to Sexual Positions
Unleash Your Potential: A Guided Journal Powered by AI Insights
Whispers of the Enchanted Grove

Cosmic Pleasures: An Astrological Guide to Sexual Kinks
369, 12 Manifestation Journal

Whisper of the nocturne journal(blank journal for writing or drawing)

The Boogey Book

Locked In Reflection: A Chastity Journey Through Locktober

Generating Wealth Quickly:

How to Generate $100,000 in 24 Hours

Star Magic: Harness the Power of the Universe

The Flatulence Chronicles: A Fart Journal for Self-Discovery

The Doctor and The Death Moth

Seize the Day: A Personal Seizure Tracking Journal

The Ultimate Boogeyman Safari: A Journey into the Boogie World and Beyond

Whispers of Samhain: 1,000 Spells of Love, Luck, and Lunar Magic: Samhain Spell Book

Apophis's guides:

Witch's Spellbook Crafting Guide for Halloween

<u>Frost & Flame: The Enchanted Yule Grimoire of 1000 Winter Spells</u>

<u>The Ultimate Boogey Goo Guide & Spooky Activities for Halloween Fun</u>

Harmony of the Scales: A Libra's Spellcraft for Balance and Beauty

The Enchanted Advent: 36 Days of Christmas Wonders

Nightmare Mansion: The Labyrinth of Screams

Harvest of Enchantment: 1,000 Spells of Gratitude, Love, and Fortune for Thanksgiving

The Boogey Chronicles: A Journal of Nightly Encounters and Shadowy Secrets

The 12 Days of Financial Freedom: A Step-by-Step Christmas Countdown to Transform Your Finances

Sigil of the Eternal Spiral Blank Journal

A Christmas Feast: Timeless Recipes for Every Meal

Cosmic Sales: The Astrological Guide to Black Friday Shopping
Legends of the Corn Mother and Other Harvest Myths
Whispers of the Harvest: The Corn Mother's Journal
The Evergreen Spellbook
The Doctor Meets the Boogeyman
The White Witch of Rose Hall's SpellBook
The Gingerbread Golem's Shadow: A Study in Sweet Darkness
The Gingerbread Golem Codex: An Academic Exploration of Sweet Myths
The Gingerbread Golem Grimoire: Sweet Magicks and Spells for the Festive Witch
The Curse of the Gingerbread Golem
10-minute Christmas Crafts for kids
<u>Christmas Crisis Solutions: The Ultimate Last-Minute Survival Guide</u>
Gingerbread Golem Recipes: Holiday Treats with a Magical Twist
The Infinite Key: Unlocking Mystical Secrets of the Ages
Enchanted Yule: A Wiccan and Pagan Guide to a Magical and Memorable Season
Dinosaurs of Power: Unlocking Ancient Magick
Astro-Dinos: The Cosmic Guide to Prehistoric Wisdom
Gallifrey's Yule Logs: A Festive Doctor Who Cookbook
The Dino Grimoire: Secrets of Prehistoric Magick
The Gift They Never Knew They Needed
The Gingerbread Golem's Culinary Alchemy: Enchanting Recipes for a Sweetly Dark Feast
A Time Lord Christmas: Holiday Adventures with the Doctor
Krampusproofing Your Home: Defensive Strategies for Yule
Silent Frights: A Collection of Christmas Creepypastas to Chill Your Bones
Santa Raptor's Jolly Carnage: A Dino-Claus Christmas Tale
Prehistoric Palettes: A Dino Wicca Coloring Journey
The Christmas Wishkeeper Chronicles

The Micro-Mastery Method: Transform Your Skills in Just Minutes a Day

Reclaiming Time: How to Live More by Doing Less

Chronovore: The Eternal Nexus

The Mind Reset: Unlocking Your Inner Peace in a Chaotic World

Confidence Code: Building Unshakable Self-Belief

Baby the Vampire Terrier

Baby the Vampire Terrier's Christmas Adventure

Celestial Streams: The Content Creator's Astrology Manual

The Wealth Whisperer: Unlocking Abundance with Everyday Actions

The Energy Equation: Maximize Your Output Without Burning Out

The Happiness Algorithm: Science-Backed Steps to Joyful Living

If you want solar for your home go here: https://www.harborso-lar.live/apophisenterprises/

Get Some Tarot cards: https://www.makeplayingcards.com/sell/apophis-occult-shop

Get some shirts: https://www.bonfire.com/store/apophis-shirt-emporium/

Instagrams:
@apophis_enterprises,
@apophisbookemporium,
@apophisscardshop
Twitter: @apophisenterpr1
Tiktok:@apophisenterprise
Youtube: @sg1fan23477, @FiresideRetreatKingdom
Hive: @sg1fan23477
CheeLee: @SG1fan23477

Podcast: Apophis Chat Zone: https://open.spotify.com/show/
5zXbrCLEV2xzCp8ybrfHsk?si=fb4d4fdbdce44dec

Newsletter: https://apophiss-newsletter-27c897.beehiiv.com/

If you want to support me or see posts of other projects that I have come over to: **<u>buymeacoffee.com/mpetchinskg</u>**
I post there daily several times a day

Get your Dinowicca or Christmas themed digital products, especially Santa Raptor songs and other musics. Here: **https://sg1fan23477.gumroad.com**

Apophis Yuletide Digital has not only digital Christmas items, but it will have all things with Dinowicca as well as other Digital products.